MW00532221

Money
Is a
Spirit
Your Economy Within

By Dr. Paula A. Price

Flaming Vision Publications
Tulsa, Oklahoma

Unless otherwise indicated, all scriptural quotations are from the King James Version of the Bible. Scripture verses marked NIV are taken from the Holy Bible, New International Version, © 1973, 1978, 1984 by the International Bible Society. Used by permission of Zondervan Publishing House.

Money Is a Spirit: Your Economy Within
Flaming Vision Publications
Tulsa, Oklahoma 74136
ISBN 1-886288-10-0

© 2003 by Dr. Paula A. Price. All rights reserved.
Reproduction of text in whole or in part without the express written consent of the author is not permitted and is unlawful according to the 1976 United States Copyright Act.

Printed in the United States of America

CONTENTS

Money Is A Spirit because its Creator is Spirit; God Is Spirit. John 4:24.

But thou shalt remember the LORD thy God: for it is he that giveth thee power to get wealth, that he may establish his covenant which he sware unto thy fathers, as it is this day. KJV Deuteronomy 8:18

MAMMON: Of Chaldean origin, the word expresses a confidence, and figuratively stands for wealth personified. Seen in the Greek as *mammonas*, its negative connotations is well earned as avarice, the deification of money, property and wealth, summarily understood as mammon, became rooted in idol worship and idolatrous service to pagan deities. See *The Prophet's Dictionary* by Dr. Paula A. Price for what is said of these ancient spirits.

The Greek form of *mammon* is Syriac or Aramaic (Chaldean*) and gives its meanings as "money," "riches," "property," and "worldly goods," or "profit." In general use it was presented as "the personification of riches bestowed and administrated by an evil spirit or deity." From about 1500 the word in English indicates "the evil influence of wealth." The word is not used in the Old Testament.

In the New Testament, it is used only by Jesus in Matthew 6:24; and Luke 16:9, 11, 13. In the Sermon on the Mount Jesus said, "Ye cannot serve God and mammon." He meant that no one could be a slave of God and worldly wealth at the same time. The undivided concentration of mind to getting money is incompatible with wholehearted devotion to God and to His service (Col. 3:5).

In the parable of the unjust steward (Luke 16:1-13), Jesus commended the steward's foresight, not his method. His object was to point out how one may best use wealth, tainted or otherwise, with a view to the future. *Excerpted from Holman Bible Dictionary *Ray Robbins.*

Linking mammon to the ancient world of Babylon, which was founded by Nimrod, can explain how and why mammon came to be designated as a person over what it is accepted as today. Removing the persona aspect of the word, and calling it an influence masks its spiritual and eternal principalic authority, nature and control in the world. It is from this meaning that the title of this book was derived.

Note: The Bible uses *Chaldea (ns), (Neo-) Babylonia (ns)* interchangeably (See Ezekiel. 1:3, RSV, NIV; 12:13, NIV). *Some author amplifications added.*

Please Note: There are lecture CD's to go with this text.
They may be ordered at www.drpaulaprice.com

4

Preface

The era of Revelation 3:7-11 is dawning upon us as the false, sin ridden economic systems of the world begin to collapse. Many fortunes will be lost, and the door for millions to become or remain rich will be forever closed. As foretold by our Savior, the world shaking God has been promising for some time is barreling down on us, and those who do not know Him or belong to Him will find out what it means to be standing upon sinking sand. Layoffs, business closings, and job insecurity can have you panicking about your future if you believe it to be in anyone's hands but the Almighty. If, however, you see what you earned not as the result of someone's good graces but as the product of what is in you then your confidence will not be shaken.

It has been said that wise and wealthy people would choose health and strength over their riches if they had to give up one or the other. The reason for this is that they know the secret to their wealth is not what they possess but what is in them. They know that if they have their health and strength, what they did once they could easily do again because what made them rich was what they came into the world with, not what they acquired. What they acquired is secondary to their real commodity, which began with skill, knowledge, acumen and guts.

Scripture says that there is a chosen group set aside by God the Father to harvest in the midst of tragedy, to prosper in the wake of sorrow, and to abound in an era of severe global lack. The era will be much like the time of Joseph under Pharaoh and Paul during Agabus' prophecy in Acts

11:28; so these times will require people to be shrewd, insightful, and astute.

Revelation 3:10 says that there is a time of severe testing coming upon the whole earth, and only those who have held fast and persevered in Jesus' truth and integrity will escape it. This book is written for them. Although its wisdom has great merit for you and me today, its value will be seen as miniscule in comparison to that day of global testing coming to try all those dwelling on the face of the earth. It is not far off, so now is the time to get it in your spirit that money (the one major loss millions will suffer at that time) is a spirit, and because it is a spirit, you who belong to Jesus Christ can generate and replenish it nearly at will.

CHAPTER ONE
Getting Acquainted with Mammon

That mammon (money/wealth) is a spirit is one of the first and most profound truths the Lord released to me about wealth. This revelation has been a long time coming if you, like me, need its wisdom to break the cycles of poverty and lack in your life. I promise that if you have the faith of a mustard seed, as our Savior said, you will certainly tap into this reality and never again struggle to get rich, fail to meet your needs, or leave the planet never knowing financial stability in your life. The transformation starts with accepting that money is a spirit. You will see this statement repeated again and again throughout your reading. I repeat it in order to establish its pulsing truth in you and to break every chain and shackle of debt, lack and poverty by getting you to change your present money thinking and thought-talk.

This revelation, better yet awareness of truth, started showing itself in my understanding about 1997. By 1998, nearly a year later, this truth was deeply implanted in my soul; though scarcely did I know or realize the power of its wisdom and insight. God was entrusting to me a staggering truth and privilege. Understanding that anything divine must find its way to the human, I recognized that I was about to learn His secrets to wealth's stronghold, systems and mysteries. The secrets I was to learn would certainly translate me into the spheres of God's financial abundance. As any good teacher would, the Lord started with the basics. The first class was one of discovery. I was to become convinced that before all else, money is a spirit because God, its Creator, is spirit (Jesus' words in John 4:23-24) and everything we see has a spiritual origin and prototype governing its manifestation in the earth. Everything means everything, and that includes money and mammon.

All God made pertaining to that resourceful commodity called mammon (money or wealth) God created along with all else He did: spirit first, since that is the raw material of His invisible creation, making money's origins *spirit* and not *material*. In addition, it makes mammon (money/wealth) eternal before it ever was a temporal thing. What all this means is that money must first be arrested and captured in the spirit before it can render its services and transmit its fruit to our natural world. We on earth in human form cannot hope to harness, attract, and gather the spirit of wealth created by the Almighty if we ignore the fact that mammon (money or wealth) is a spirit and must first obey the laws and government of the spirit realm before being subjected to those of this world.

Since the beginnings of earthly civilizations and communities, people have sought the secret to this mysterious and elusive *essentia* – that vital something that no one on earth can do without, of human life. Over the millennia of humanity's existence, they have seen money make itself known to our natural world but still struggle to grasp how it does so. How is it that some are born into it and others die laboring for it? What makes money a servant to one and an archenemy to another? How do I get this vitality of human existence to want to abide in my life abundantly, many ask? Where does it all begin?

Money usually invites itself into a person's life through need, which happens quite early. Until need arises, people have little awareness of money's power and capacity. Once money introduces need to someone, it then presents its problematic side, lack. Lack is the taunting side of mammon. It surfaces to teach the needy that neither lack nor deprivation wins money. Money's message is clear: "If you want me to supply you, you must approach me by the set rules I was created to demand. If not, all your tears, loss, lack and suffering will not win me." Specific rules and influences get money's attention and release its treasuries. Until you discover them, you stumble in your need and remain locked in the chamber of lack. Here is one way it works: "I need this or that, but I don't see a way to get it." Money trains you to respect it by teaching you to react to need with panic, fear, and confusion. "I need, but I cannot see how to meet my need." This class can go on for decades, if not a lifetime. As yet, money has not shown you its other side. It is the one that disciplines you in the sometimes frustrating, but not to be forgotten lessons. Money chastises you until you realize that need is neither its master nor its suitor. If you rely on need alone to put money in your hands, you will suffer a very long time.

Money defies your petitions, laughs at your need, and determinedly does not play fair. It does not go to the one who needs it most; it responds to the one who desires and compels it into his or her sphere of life. If you don't fit that category, then pleas, lack and calamity run rampant as the spirit of money turns a deaf ear to your plights. Your suffering actually works against you during your training years as you give money the excuse it needs to ignore you

9

and go to the one who has somehow proven he or she wants it more, who respects it more than you. Money seeks those that will celebrate its presence in their lives, preserve its laws, and see that it always gets a chance to multiply. Sounds very much like a person, doesn't it? Well it is a person; it is the Person of the Lord Jesus Christ in whom Creator God hid all His treasures and wealth. Just look at Christ's attitude toward money and wealth in the scriptures from His parables about multiplication and increase in the following passages of scripture. In studying them, you see that our loving, humble and meek Savior recognizes that loss and lack are not residents of His Father's kingdom. Read His parable of the talents and the pound (mina) and notice that the one who gave Him the greatest increase on His investment was the one He trusted and rewarded with the most. Need did not figure into the equation. See Matthew 25:15-21 and Luke 19:13-26.

In John 6:39 our Savior assured His Father before leaving the earth that of all He was entrusted with He lost nothing. After feeding thousands on more than one occasion, He instructed His disciples to gather up the leftovers so nothing was lost. These three examples say well what heaven feels about money and wealth. Since John 6:63 says that Jesus' words are spirit and life, we may well understand that money is spirit, for that is the composition of God's invisible worlds. As you read on, you will find why and how the spirit of mammon exhibits all the characteristics society has come to accept as personhood.

Money has very old and very formidable guards to protect it from the needy and to seduce the greedy. Why did our Savior say in Mark 14:7 that we would always have the poor with us? Why did He want us to search the scriptures and study the word to find out about money? The answer to these questions will help you identify those few selected to easily inherit, access, and plunder money's secret treasuries. Learning the answers also tell you the grounds upon which others (chosen over you to learn its secrets) tap into its eternally hidden mysteries. Although you need money and would do so much good with it, you will see why money seems utterly disinterested in your visions and dreams. Grasping the reality that mammon is a spirit begins to help you easily tap into those hidden riches in secret places which the Lord Almighty promised to king Cyrus centuries before he was born (see Isaiah chapter 45).

Throughout history, the secret to making, saving, and wisely using or multiplying money has preoccupied thinkers, teachers, laborers and financiers alike. Centuries of people have wondered what makes one person successfully wealthy and leaves others in abject poverty, regardless of how sweet, honest, or generous they were to others in life. What all these past cultures overlooked and most modern people today don't realize is that money is a spirit. That is the initial part of its secret riches and wealth. It is an invisible, intelligent, and protective agency whose disbursements may only be had by those who dare defy its hallowed doors to conquer its barriers. The spirit of money deliberately refuses early access and, ideally, lifetime access to its hidden hordes if you have not been born into them. "But where are those hordes?" you ask. They are in the realm of the spirit, which is why you can see them in your sleep; which is why when you dream and pray or focus on money for long periods, you envision it in a world and place you seem to be shut out of and forbidden to enter.

The Bible tells the New Creation church that they are "hidden in Christ in whom is hid all the treasures of wisdom and knowledge." Wealth and riches are hid in Jesus Christ in the Creator's realm, and mammon, their tangible instruments, are on earth to misguide and confuse people into pursuing money's form instead of its

> Having completed His assignment given by the Father, the Lord Jesus successfully gathered into one what He owned but was robbed of and retrieved from the forces of darkness. As the Author of all things, Jesus is the lone embodiment of all the Creator's wealth as His firstborn Son and Savior of the world and all creation.

spiritual substance in its earthly appearance. See Proverbs 22:4, 16; 23:5.

For nearly 20 years, I explored the scriptures for the key to its *ploutos*[1] treasuries only to find out that it is hid in Jesus Christ, God's Co-Creator and our Redeemer. Nonetheless, there is another side of the story, and that is where money is hid in the world. (It is confined to the treasuries of the Lord Jesus Christ where it, because it is spirit, began.) By the way, you should know that mammon occupies two spheres of existence with rules for each. The amount and demands of money are important to know depending upon the sphere you occupy.

The Creator's wealth streams, the book of Proverbs tells us, are in His kingdom, which one must be a naturalized citizen of to even qualify for it. His kingdom is the eternal sphere of money, whose riches far supersede that of our

---

[1] *Ploutos* is the Greek word for *riches*.

sphere. Money's other sphere is that of this world. In the world's sphere, the Lord has assigned certain spiritual forces to administrate and dispense His invisible wealth to those who would turn it into its natural form. The underlying truth of the two parables referred to earlier in Matthew and Luke's gospels is that *mammon*, the name the Lord Jesus used to describe the inferior monetary systems and ungodly economies of this world, makes most people victims of its callous indifference.

Proverbs 8 gives God's record of wealth's history, methods, and destiny. Here money is pictured as a woman, symbology that foretokens His New Creation church over which the Son of God Jesus Christ became head. Lady wisdom speaks of money as a resource entrusted to her care and keeping. She alone, before Jesus Christ, had the power and secrets of wealth, world dominance, and the mystery that transforms the impoverished into the prosperous and powerful.

Now having been absorbed into the body of the Lord Jesus, the new creation church places those very principles and practices in the hands of the Bride of Christ. The implications are tremendous if the church would accept its awesome charge to release wealth's counsel, obey its guidelines, and learn the work of its wisdom in this world. The Lord Jesus deposited such wisdom in His church to reward billions with trillions for millennia. Accessing the sphere of money would benefit the church whose standard for dispensing it is radically different from that of the world. This is the reason this world's monetary guards fight Christians so fiercely for it. Christ's parable in Matthew 21:33-40 fitly applies. Our Proverbs reference further establishes money's spiritual roots. Economically speaking, wisdom equals money; therefore, mammon (money/wealth) belongs to wisdom.

Moreover, wisdom and wealth are like your first and last names. One without the other would just not quite identify you. While the Bible does speak about sudden riches, dishonest gain, and wealth without right, God promises their joys are short lived. At death, such riches are lost to or wasted on the posterity of those who once possessed it. Therefore, it is impossible to retain or multiply money without wisdom, and that is another of its primitive secrets.

Chapter Two
The Rules of Money

Money has rules, protocols, and strategies that all collectively lend themselves to its dynamics. They partner with money in its frustrating habit of releasing itself only to those who force its disbursements into their lives. This is somewhat the way wisdom deals with her treasures, promotions, and benefits. Money has devoted guardians that react to defend its barricades every time you take steps to appropriate its treasuries. Money will punish sloth, vindicate waste, and judge recklessness. On the positive side, money's protective guardians are [1] faith and fear; [2] diligence and determination; [3] willingness and work; [4] righteousness and risk; [5] skill and shrewdness; [6] sacrificial service; [7] seed sowing and harvest; [8] giving and generosity; [9] and replenishment and reward. Regardless of their order, before you can experience a lasting breakthrough in the area of money you will have to spend a good amount of time in each one of these domains in order to learn your lessons well.

1. **Faith** is how God created mammon, so its conqueror must be as solid in the same kind and degree of faith. Fear prevents faith and is the first place we encounter money's resistance. Conquering deep-rooted fears concerning money, being rich, or meeting its requirements alone meets the demands of money. Fearing money is the typical person's response. They need money, and it has taunted them so much over

the years that they knuckle under its resistance just for the sake of peace and merely to get out of the fight. Here is where they surrender and anoint their money needs with panic and anxiety instead of the characteristic faith that brought it into existence in the first place. Money will trick you into thinking that it and confidence are archrivals. You either believe that you should have it and that it is provided by the Lord to be your servant, or you believe that you must serve it to have just enough to get by without the struggle of the rat race.

2. **Diligence and determination** say that casual, haphazard efforts toward acquiring money will not do. Money's pursuers must actively respect what wealth requires in order to be apprehended. Money expects to be respected, courted, and treated with regard. You must know and honor its boundaries in order to relegate it to a servant instead of a master. Those who handle larges sums of money, access and accumulate it seemingly at will approach it with this mindset. They are the ruler, and mammon is the servant; it is in the world to serve them. They believe this to the point of becoming almost cocky, yet strangely it does work. Keeping this view in godly perspective gives you the same advantage. Money wants you to celebrate the hard work (mental or otherwise) that went into your winning its contests by being a good steward over what you have been rewarded. Everyday you are expected to compete with lack, loss, and misfortune by diligently handling

and multiplying whatever sums of money the Lord entrusts to you.

3. **Willingness** and **Work** are money's fundamental demands. Regardless of what kind of effort brought you your funds, you are expected to recognize the laws of return attached to money and wealth. Something must be exerted and exercised in order for money to free its holdings even a little bit. Many people make the mistake of giving a giant push to get what they need with the intent of kicking back to indolence once it is over. Money is smarter than that and will chasten you until you realize that its possessions are a lifetime effort. Laziness is a hedge against wealth and success. The less you are willing to put into acquiring your wealth, the less money regards you as a viable contender for it.

Money has a divine command to punish the slothful, the lazy, and the indolent. Even if the work you put forth for money is mental or spiritual, the command, according to Proverbs, is that money rewards the diligent. This does not mean only the hard working; diligence goes much deeper than that. It calls for attentiveness, persistence, perseverance, and acumen to see that what is produced is done correctly and is worthy of economic reward.

4. **Righteousness** and **Risk** tell us that money may eke out its blessings from time to time under ungodly circumstances, but its outpourings do not stay long where they fall. In addition, risk is a constant in every endeavor to earn money. Often without knowing or agreeing to it, money gets you to go out

on a limb to sufficiently meet your needs and repeats the process to continue supplying you in the future. Need establishes the lack of money or its deficit in your life. Going after money, however, does not, in itself, assure you will come back with what you went after or needed. God's word has much to say about righteousness and lasting wealth and riches. It also says that the costs of risks must be counted. See Jesus' words in Luke 14:28-32.

5. **Skill** and **Shrewdness** speak to your competitive ability to earn money; it explains the use of the word *earnings* in relation to your pursuing and acquiring it. Shrewdness says you have the ability to keep and increase what you earn. The idea is that "just enough to get by" will not net you the measure of wealth you desire, no matter how much you try to "faith it in" or to put an emotional demand upon it.

6. **Sacrifice** and **Service** say that, strangely, mammon asks the same thing of you as anything else in your life. It too requires you to give of yourself and to do for others. The only difference is that what you do for others for money can bring immediate reward; with mammon that is not always the case. Getting significant money requires you to give beyond what is normal for you to give or do often without a hint of some immediate reward. You just do it because you know the laws of creation and that persistence and perseverance must yield their return on your efforts. Naturally, one does not merely sacrifice to themselves, so the service elements say that you must render it to others in return for something of value.

7. **Seed Sowing** and **Harvest** is the constant that shows the possession of money is invariably the product of something given in exchange for it.

   People with a destiny of wealth learn early that something for nothing is not the way of the world, but those who do not believe that can surely give up any idea of having sufficient money and wealth at their disposal. In addition, the reality is that money operates on a pure exchange system. This is the most enduring truth about money and wealth: sowing guarantees a harvest. When they sow, they wait for the harvest because such people know that money and its treasures respect the laws of seedtime and harvest.

   When things seem to take forever to materialize, these people resort to the faith stance and accept that what was sown has to bear fruit, so they wait for the appointed time for their harvest. The reason is the law of the spirit realm. Whatever is brought into this world must clothe itself with a body. Spiritual manifestations in this world only prove their presence and usefulness through some natural or physical means. So, while money is a spirit, you must do what it takes to give your portion of it a body and power. "And that which thou sowest, thou sowest not that body that shall be, but bare grain, it may chance of wheat, or of some other grain: But God giveth it a body as it hath pleased him, and to every seed his own body" (1 Corinthians 15:37, 38).

8. **Giving** and **Generosity** is a staunch requirement of mammon. The giving and the generous are sure to

have much. This goes along with the sowing and seedtime for harvest, but extends it from more than labor and service to being there for people when they are in need. Scripture has much to say about extending one's hand to the poor, giving to those who ask, and similar statements. The New Testament adds that sowing material things is a direct correlation to reaping spiritually and vice versa.

9. **Replenishment** and **Reward** go with the Lord's words to His created male and female in Genesis 1:27. Among the other Creator endowment edicts spoken to them, the Lord God says to them to "replenish" the earth. This is a strange statement that induces one into thinking that the vast creative works of the Lord on earth were more of a restoration than a first creation. Still, it goes without saying that what is consumed must be replenished, and the need for replenishment is a result of having been rewarded with increase for one's efforts. To see the first or early installments of money in one's life as a single automatic event that takes care of all future needs, especially if it is a large sum, is short sighted.

Mammon expects to build a productive relationship with you and presents you with little victory tests along the way to its treasuries to assure that you have sufficient skill to release it and the wisdom to retain what has been released to you. In a strange encouraging move, mammon seems to take notice of you and respond to your compliance with its nine-point plan. Here you get another invitation which entices you to go further, to not stop altogether

20

as if the mere drop in the bucket you just received is the end of the journey. A response such as the above will surely withhold or delay future releases until you learn better.

Chapter Three
The Race is Not to the Swift

I cannot tell you how many people who, after laboring and enduring for a long time before their blessing came, have fallen prey to the tactic of overwhelming fatigue. Far too often, people allow weariness to set in during their strenuous journey and receive less than what is available for them. Money's aggressive guardians seduce such people into falling back and settling for the current windfall without regard to what the spirit realm still held in store for them. They forsook wealth in favor of a mere monetary breakthrough. Most people have no idea that the Creator stocked His planet with each creature's allocated economy stored up in the spirit realm. Everyone born on the planet has a divine portion of potential to produce, although many of them never tap into it during their lifetime. Each person's Creator gifts and talents can carry them into the hidden treasuries of creation if they just learn the secrets of doing so.

An inward knowledge of the spiritual monetary portion God set aside for them can urge people to press to retrieve and materialize, in our world, what they were born into as humans. Most people instinctively know this is done through hard work, skill, wisdom, training, and endurance. It does not matter who it is; there is an eternal economic reserve in store for everyone born into the world, and redemption and religious service have little to do with whether or not one accesses it. Here is what the Creator means about that which is laid up for the wicked and the just. There is an inheritance in the Adamic lineage, which is distributed by those forces assigned to see to their distributions, and there is an inheritance that goes all the way through eternity for those who are in Jesus Christ. The Bible mentions inheritance nearly 240 times. This indicates its importance to the Almighty, and yet the subject is scarcely touched or understood by His Son's church.

Unsaved souls have one treasury, and those who receive Jesus Christ and His indwelling Spirit have another more enduring and infinitely lavish one. Redemption was an extravagant plan, costing the Most High considerably. Consequently, its reward must be equivalent to, if not exceeding, the others since eternity's riches are to supply the Lord's offspring forever in His world without end. That treasury is to sustain a race of people not obliged to die for the infinity it takes to discover Christ's eternal wealth and learn to harvest and multiply it forever. Such a generation's pursuit of wealth, then, in all its forms and on every plane in the timeless world has much to learn about God, how He does things, and where His eternal creatures harvest, acquire, and exchange their gifts and talents for *supramaterial* gain and advancement. Riches mean something altogether different to those who inhabit eternity. That is why it is important to recognize that mammon (money/wealth) is a spirit.

Speaking of the generations, another thing to know about mammon is that it is also tied to genetics and genealogy. Family lines are often endowed because of a patriarchal covenant, a champion member's reward, or a redeemed ancestor's pleasing life before the Lord. If a person dies before the reward for their deeds or service to God was received, it remains in the line to bless those of later generations. This fact explains why some people seem born to inherit what they have neither sown nor pursued. This spiritual custom encourages parents to store up an inheritance for their later generation. Proverbs 13:22 agrees and says that the righteous leave an inheritance to their children's children.

Money as a spirit is tied to many prefixed variables. For instance, as we have said, money is tied to genetics and genealogy and linked to geography; it is a foregone conclusion that some locales are richer in natural resources than others. Likewise, money is connected to nationality. Some nations, because of their geography, are more endowed than others with wealth building and income producing ideas and natural resources to turn into wealth. The more the light of God shines on the land, the more brilliant its people will be. When the land ceases to regard its Creator and its laws, the light grows dim and stagnation takes over.

Moreover, money is governed by wisdom irrespective of redemption because its superintendence belongs to the supernatural beings that administrate it for the natural beings they oversee as assigned by the Creator. The Bible has much to say about spiritual rulers, principalities, thrones, and dominions in the invisible realm who are responsible for what is produced or manifested in this world. The Bible also teaches that a spiritual territory governs every geographic location on the earth. The prophetic revelations of Daniel and Zechariah make this plain to us. Thus the wealth and riches hidden in the lands

24

are dispensed based on the Creator's heavenly allotment plan. See Deuteronomy 32:8 and Ezekiel 28:14-28.

Superior celestial beings hold sway over mammon and when and how it is dispensed. Those meant to inherit an abundance of it generally receive both training and visitations from these beings so they know that it was not merely due to their own efforts that they were made rich, but because of the superior powers that chose them according to the directives of God. Thus, the acquisition of money is first a spiritual matter where its invisible authorities must be cajoled or appeased into releasing it. According to their Creator's distribution plan, these spiritual managers dole out wealth and riches based on the parameters just described. However, since money is a spirit, begin to ask yourself what, in fact, is distributed.

Being forced to rely on some invisible and presumably detached being for an opportunity at creation's riches can initially sound bleak until you remember that Jesus Christ, money's Co-Creator, died and rose again to join all things together (to reconcile them) in one under the sole domain of His Father who in turn placed it under His Son's control. See Ephesians 1:10 and Colossians 1:15-20. "All things" in this instance includes what is seen and unseen, heavenly and earthly, spiritual and natural, and all that includes money to greater explain why and how it is spirit. Prior to the finished work of Jesus Christ on the cross, money was irrationally and often unjustly granted at the whim of those prejudicial forces of nature that sought to reward their wicked offspring with their spiritual blessings. Selfishly they enriched and impoverished people under their dominion at will. Ephesians 1:3 says that Jesus reversed this by blessing His offspring with every spiritual blessing in the heavenly places. What does that mean except that there is a permanent reversal of how the wealth of creation is bestowed as a result of Calvary and our Lord's resurrection? All this adds to the reality that mammon is a *spirit*; it is not and was never intended to become a *god*.

Fallen angels, devils, and humans made it so by devious seductions. Sadly, humans did so to their own hurt. Originally as a spirit, mammon was meant to be unearthed through people's discovery of the Creator's riches deposited in the planet and in its people. They were to find out how the planet's natural resources could meet their needs, solve their problems, and improve the quality of their lives.

Since not all people have the same talents and abilities, those gifted in one area could harvest themselves and the earth to employ technological skills to offer to the rest in exchange for something of value for what they lacked. That is how it all began. As people began to populate the earth, their needs surfaced. Correspondingly, Creator wisdom activated in them and flourished as well. One person's natural wisdom solved the daily existence problems of others by inventing ways to help them meet their needs. Over time the practice gave way to industry as more and more needs were met and more and more people discovered their natural gifts and talents for doing so. Soon demands grew and so supply increased accordingly until we come down the line to today where industries were born, consumerism took hold, and their very crude starts turned into the modern marvels and wonders of today's and tomorrow's worlds.

Chapter Four
Before There was Cash

I n the beginning, there was no such thing as money as we know it, at least not as currency. Early civilization's monetary system was quite crude and the idea of paper currency and coins had yet to emerge. They simply used whatever was valued in the tribe and accepted as universally valuable to the whole as an exchange instrument. For some that may have been stones, animal bones or skins, prized trophies, or livestock. However, transferring livestock and other oversized valuables became too burdensome; this motivated the invention of an easier exchange system. Natural objects such as stones, for instance, once representing their monetary system, eventually evolved into the sophisticated financial institutions we use today. Back when things were being discovered and developed, money as we know it now did not exist, just needs and exchanges resulting from one person's products being needed and exchanged used by another. As things progressed, expedience gave way to sophistication and harvested treasures were transformed into products that necessitated the creation of currency in place of the animals and such, which initially served as payment for goods and services. These explanations give further credence to the fact that money is a spirit. People under this arrangement, however, began to be closed out of the legitimate right to control and distribute mammon for themselves as banks and similar financial institutions took power. As such, citizens became pawns to those higher powers whose authority over wealth manipulated them merciless for it.

Down through the ages things have not changed, and people are still being held sway due to their need and desire for money and the fundamental inability to acquire it. Abuses and excesses have usurped wisdom and merit so that money appears to be utterly out of the reach of those not favored by the systems of this world. However, as I have said, money is a spirit and I will reiterate it throughout this writing to pound it in your heart and head solidly enough to shatter all your suffocating myths and fears concerning it. Money has two Creator-assigned agendas; like sin, it is to be conquered and ruled over by those of humanity that know its role in life. The other agenda is to make victims and slaves of those too foolish to discover its truths; those whose foolish ideas and fantasies about money doom them to a life or servitude, lack, and poverty.

After being brought into subjection, God's intent was that money be used to equitably prosper its holders and their communities and fulfill His Creator edict to be fruitful and multiply. People who understand how to fearlessly unseal its mysteries instinctively grasp and operate these two aims of mammon and wealth. As a spirit, money is forced by its own hidden rules designed to withhold itself from those who dismiss its undeclared premises for success. Furthermore, it is administrated by extremely ancient and highly intelligent beings who have no personal stake in releasing it to those who will not yield a return on their dispensations*. Remember these foundations as the basis for[i] the Lord Jesus' parables of the talents and mina in the gospels referred to earlier. A balanced perception helps us to

28

see that money and mammon are not evil in themselves. Jesus' parables were **not** to voice that they were and therefore to be shunned by all who profess holiness and righteousness to God. What our Lord said was that you cannot **serve** God and mammon. To those of His day, it made perfect sense, since doing so would put Israel's God in conflict with the gods of this world. In saying this, the Lord did not condemn the need for or possession of money. Rather He wanted us to keep our priorities straight while we still acquired the wealth His shed blood freed us to earn and use to His glory. Mammon, back then, was seen as a god itself (for some today it still is). Jesus wanted to make sure that His people continually kept His God as their source and viewed money as merely a resource. Even when He made statements about the rich man and the kingdom of God, His thought was that those chosen to be rich in this world had the grave responsibility of keeping heaven and Christ's redemption as the most important of their business transaction in this life. They would be faced with choosing the Lord more often than a poorer person because money's spirit in this world presents itself as a god; a god that requires everything that the God of gods condemns to be won or retained. Deceit, theft, duplicity, and immorality are all the things the god of this world demands in return for access to mammon's coffers. The Father and God of the Lord Jesus is the extreme opposite and thus puts the rich of the world at risk or, at the least, to the test of losing all their wealth to remain or prove their faithfulness to the Savior. It is under these conditions that the Lord declared that it is hard—not impossible—for the rich man to enter and remain in the kingdom of God.

The wisdom behind this world's monetary systems was intended to give humanity insight on how God reproduces Himself and His treasures and uses them to prosper and benefit others—an ideal often lost or perverted by the ilk of greed. Nonetheless, that does not mean money's pursuit is to be abandoned forever by the redeemed as the wicked of the world use it to rule ruthlessly over the righteous, the meek, or the less enriched. The Bible speaks repeatedly about the Lord's concern for the poor and His condemnation of the rich for exploiting them. The cross and the new birth were meant to include God's deliverance of His powers of wealth and prosperity into the hands of the righteous to halt the cruelty that sinners commit on the weak because of their lack.

As a spirit, mammon has a will, a persona and emotions that give it all the features of personhood. Here is why people who have and grasp the concepts of money exhibit similar attitudes and beliefs concerning it. It seems that their behaviors facilitate their ability to boldly pursue and acquire money and remain undaunted when it appears to resist their efforts or slip through their fingers. Perhaps they know that what they are dealing with is not the currency, but the agencies responsible for administrating it in the earth and in creation's spheres (each of which has its own stock treasury for the benefit of humanity). Being a spirit, mammon is still not as impersonal as we are led to believe. God oversees its superintendence and manages its staff so that mammon responds, even if involuntarily to those who adequately petition it or apply its rules of distribution. Its objectives react according to prescribed apportionment guidelines similar to how electricity and the other earthly elements and forces respond when due diligence is put into effect to compel their supply to and in our world. While fire does not have the power to discriminate, when its laws are violated it does respond to active, counteractive, or proactive demands to appear and perform. It may not have the license to decide to skip one person and consume another, but fire can be manipulated according to its laws. The same is true for the other elements and resources stocking the planet and their spheres of earthly provision. In like manner, mammon responds and reacts to attract or repel those who respect or disregard its principles. It administrates its treasures based on the Creator's divine distribution plan.

We have already established that wisdom is the principal thing in relation to mammon. Previously we also listed nine requirements that contribute to our successful quest for money and wealth in this life. Peculiarly nine is the number of the Spirit, the Holy Spirit and coincidentally it is the same number of months it takes to birth a child into the world. What makes this relevant to our discussion is the premise of this book; money is a spirit, and that being the case, spiritual wisdom is just as important to obtaining it as natural wisdom. Bringing something into this world from the invisible one is synonymous with spiritual birthing.

To get into this world, money must be birthed according to those nine requirements discussed earlier. That is the only way *spiritual mammon* can take on its natural form and be of service to us. What is its bodily form, you ask? It is the form of cash or currency, or other instruments this world uses to convert mammon into money and money into wealth and possessions. Before its instruments of transaction appear, money is an idea; at the least, it is intangible. It is the physical paper, coins, and such that cause mammon to become what we see. We buy and sell with these tools, called instruments.

By now, you see firsthand why and how money is a spirit. Deceptively, it has forced your battles with it to target the wrong enemy. If you are like most people, pursuing money means tracking and discovering ways to increase your cash flow. Spiritually and eternally speaking, that negates your capacity to get wealth because you have been more or less paper chasing. Here is why. Those yet to be enlightened are taught to measure money in terms of what is in their pockets, what is in their bank accounts, what they own and owe. By the time these things manifest, the spiritual flow that manufactured them is exhausted. In short, once they are consumed, if nothing replenishes them in the spirit you will be bankrupt. In God's world, natural visibility equates to spiritual expenditure. To have something appear in its physical form is to have withdrawn it from its spiritual reserves. Therefore, the world's four standards of wealth — their bank accounts, pocketbooks, property and debts — lag behind the spirit realm where its powers are produced and dispatched into our own.

How the world is taught to view, pursue and regard money then becomes its downfall, which is why its systems keep collapsing. The number four mentioned earlier, by the way, is the number of the world, and it is because of its darkness that they measure everything in physical terms. That is according to the five senses; what is seen, tasted, touched and felt is the typical standard of measurement. With no access to the Creator's light and life outside of Jesus Christ, they operate on the expended, the obsolete, and bankrupt rather than the eternal and inexhaustible. Thus they pursue wealth by pursuing its paper, disregarding what causes God's products to come and remain in their lives.

Pursuing cash as the sum of mammon can tie you up all your life, deceiving you into chasing paper money and valuating yourself by its form instead of what the Lord set aside for you in the spirit realm, where money and wealth actually begin and emanate. We who know God by His Spirit within understand better. If we took the status of Christ as the Bible presents Him (see Ephesians 2:17-23) at face value and respected our position in Him verbatim, as His body and bride, our entire spiritual climate would change our world and money would then be seen for what it is — a slave to the righteous and not its cruel fickle taskmaster. As a spirit, money is a servant to Christ Jesus our head and thus to us as His body.

Sound too simple? That's because it really is to those who have seen and thus entered the kingdom of God. If you are wrestling with accepting this pure truth in its simplicity, perhaps it is because your economic taskmaster is protecting his stockpile to keep you from your legal portion of the money supply that Creator God deposited in the earth. This common tactic deprives you from using your new creation privileges to demand him to loose it. Since God made money a spirit first, the Lord Jesus has given us His power over it along with all the works of the Father's hands in this world. Here is the essence of what Ephesians 1:18-23 and 1 John 4:17 speak to concerning the new creation church as the body of the Lord Jesus Christ.

Isaiah 11:1-5 list what may be known as the sevenfold operations of the Spirit of God; this is what rested upon the Messiah when He entered earth to fulfill His redemptive mission. However questionable this may be, it does remain that the Lord ascribed His extraordinary human power and authority to the Holy Spirit as the nature of the Savior's supernatural equipment used on assignment in this world. Heading the list of those spiritual manifestations is wisdom.

The frontrunner to the rest of the abilities the Lord Jesus employed in His divine service, wisdom is seen as the purveyor of all the Almighty cultivated and deposited in this world for our use and enrichment. That wisdom is tantamount to a bestowal of eternal enrichment is seen throughout the Proverbs.

What *etherealists* [2] see, then, as obscure aesthetic virtues, the Lord has an altogether different view concerning His Spirit and its operations, wisdom in particular. In God's mind and according to King Solomon, money is empowered by wisdom. This notably wise king actually manifested his wisdom by so enriching his land that silver and gold became commonplace possessions throughout the country. What an astounding demonstration of the link between wisdom and wealth. For the Bible's ongoing association of wisdom with money, see Proverbs 3:19 and Ecclesiastes 7:11, 12 for further comprehension. That wisdom is also a spirit may be found in Exodus 28:3; Deuteronomy 34:9; Isaiah 11:2 and Ephesians 1:17. Meanwhile 1 Corinthians 1:30 says that the Lord Jesus is made unto us wisdom; while Colossians 2:1-3 say that in God and Christ are hid all the treasures of wisdom and knowledge again equating wisdom with wealth or riches.

Treasures there speak to *"a deposit of laid up wealth stored in a secret place to be committed by appointment as a set aside portion associated with an ordained purpose."* What would you say to someone you wanted to understand this thought? Look at the key words in the explanation: a) deposit, b) laid up wealth, c) secret place, d) committed by appointment e) set aside portion f) ordained purpose. What conclusion may

---

[2] Etherealists –Those who desire only immateriality.

35

be drawn from applying these words on their own merits to mammon and its wisdom?

Treasure is a key term used sixteen times in the New Testament in relation to mammon, money, and wealth. Aside from its worldly applications, it is generously applied to the exalted ministry of our Lord Jesus Christ and His church. Jesus spoke of treasure, as being located at the seat of our hearts stating that wherever one is the other will be. (See Matthew 6:21 and 12:35-37 that link treasure as expressed above with the kingdom of heaven in the Lord's teachings). Additionally, Luke 12:33 talks about treasure being in the heavens, which makes what we chase on earth a mere facsimile in comparison, which is what everything in this world is according to the Creator. On this planet, He condemns them as corroding facsimiles. Since earth's treasures and wealth are based on physical resources devoid of the life (spiritual life) of their Maker, without fail they fade and erode over time. All these passages lead up to the reality that kingdom treasures are in the heart, and whatever is in the heart will eventually make its way into the world to take on a physical body and fulfill God's goal of imposing His spirituality on our natural world in the first place. In support of this statement just look at the New Testament word for "*riches*" and its Bible characterizations.

1. Riches of this life, Luke 8:10
2. Riches of goodness, Romans 2:4
3. Riches of God's grace, Ephesians 1:7
4. Riches of glory, Romans 9:23; Romans 9:23; Ephesians 3:16
5. Riches of this world, Romans 11:12; 1 Timothy 6:17
6. Riches of Wisdom & knowledge, Romans 11:33

7. Riches of liberty, 2 Corinthians 1:2
8. Riches of grace, Ephesians 1:7
9. Riches of Christ (unsearchable), Ephesians 3:8
10. Riches of glory in us, Ephesians 1:18
11. Riches of hope in us, Colossians 1:27
12. Riches of reproach of Christ, Hebrews 11:26
13. Corrupt riches, James 5:2
14. Lamb's riches, Revelation 5:12

In contrast, *wealth* is discussed in scripture twenty-seven times and has at least six different meanings ranging from "the force, virtue, and valor it takes to conquer obstacles" to "obtaining goods and riches," and "the self made millionaire that learned the secret of bringing wealth out of nothing;" or better yet out of the hidden treasures buried within by the Creator. Upgrading your present redemption view of money from that of an unfathomable influence to that of a spiritual person should liberate you immensely from your bondage to the impression that money is an elusive blessing meant for everyone else but you.

From now on, you have solid ground to see it for what it is instead of what it once was in the world. No longer are you shut out of its treasuries because unclean, evil spirits originally holding sway over the world's deposited wealth tries to give it to their children. That reality is no longer true for you because it all belongs to Jesus Christ who distributes it as the Father wills to His children according to their discovery and compliance with its set rules. Scripture upholds this as Paul says in 1 Corinthians1:5; 3:22.

At the top of those rules is the discovery and application of money's prescribed wisdom, divinely motivated favor, and the Lord's charges concerning it in regard to your divine purpose in life. Refer back to mammon's definition at the beginning of this book. Once you grab hold of these, you are on your way to getting that power to get wealth spoken of in Deuteronomy 8:17-18; Isaiah 48:17 to establish the Lord's covenant with you. Such a covenant must be made to rescue you from the life of poverty that you may have been born into naturally. Redemption is by covenant and to show that God performed it in your life, He prospers you to the degree that you can handle and bring glory to Him.

Poverty is an enemy, the product of the curse, and therefore is the power of another god at work in your life. The Most High Lord's covenant is one of richness, wealth, and prosperity in every area of creation. Abundance is His normal way and will for you, not lack. At the point that you accept and assimilate these truths in your soul and mind, which are already deposited in your spirit, you will be begin to capture and wield the laws of mammon to compel it to serve you as a member of the Godhead. As a member of Christ's body, you are above all principality and power and every name that is named in this world and in that which is to come. At present, two forces may be shutting you out of your dominion over money and finances; they are fear and lack of identity.

If you do not change your identity to that of Jesus Christ, you will never be eligible to exercise His authority and power over your financial situations. What you have in your new creation spirit, the deposit of the Holy Spirit, and all that He provides will stay locked inside you until you leave the planet. Once you mature in Christ you are then in a position to let His mind not only be in you as His offspring, but to also begin the first steps of excising and thus managing the massive wealth that He has hid in your vessel as part of His glorious redemption at work in you. Here is where you begin to unfold another mystery of the cross: salvation, the new birth, and Christ in you. At this point, you will begin to realize the fullness of His hope and glory in you as a result the numerous unsearchable riches of Christ.

All that you previously struggled with and labored over was for a misguided illusion in your pursuit of financial security. While it was a deliberate misguidance, it is time for you to recognize that all you seek and pursue in this life is now within you because you are filled with all the fullness of God and are the embodiment of all the fullness of the Godhead. Settle it in your heart that the kingdom of God is within you and take a moment right this minute to meditate on what that says to you, if you dare take it at face value. Just repeat this statement over and over again from your mouth: *"I am the full embodiment of the Godhead, that is the Father, the Son, and the Holy Spirit. The fullness of God – Creator God – indwells me by the Holy Spirit. As He is so am I in this world."* As you begin to just speak these words to yourself night and day, you will release the strength you need to get the rest of the story and act on the power God delivered to you to manifest the wealth He assigned to your life and posterity in the earth.

Chapter Six
Wealth Manifesting Seminar

My number two problem in ministry, in fact since my birth, was releasing the hidden something that I sensed was suffocating inside me. Perhaps as you read this book you are in that place right now. Constantly I probed my soul for it everyday to answer one crisis after another. Somehow, I knew as you probably do that greatness was buried deep within begging to get out to express itself and to impact my world. That mysterious something was my call and I know that it is your call as well. Once you recognize that God placed a calling on your life, you need to look for the cache of blessings, abilities, powers, and talents He deposited in you to provide for and finance your fulfillment of that calling. These constitute your divine treasury and are meant for you to tap into and retrieve, as you need to move His marvelous spiritual provisions into your life. In order for you to successfully retrieve this cache, you will need help and training.

While many people on the planet do not need salvation to prosper, they do need it for their prosperity to accompany them into eternity. That does not exclusively or always mean money. However, God will most often reflect His unspeakable riches in your life with money to the benefit and observation of others. From the beginning of time, people somehow knew that life under the sun was not all there was for their existence. History is full of people who amassed large wealth in their lifetimes only to discover that once they left their bodies they would have no more say over it. They had to leave it to others who probably would consume it in a moment. Over the centuries, these people have contrived numerous ways to take their wealth with them. Some choose to be buried with it as though those who covered their coffins would not first line their own coffers. Others have tried to send their wealth on journeys ahead of them by burning it in order to release their wealth's material elements from the spiritual sources. These are all statements that attest to humanity's instinctive understanding that what they make in this life remains on earth once they have departed.

On the other hand, you as God's child have another option once you accept that money is a spirit and that every natural wealth has a supernatural counterpart. Understanding this can help you to refrain from worshiping what God gives you and to realize that He bestows riches and empowers you to release and distribute His wealth as He leads. He expects you to know that you are only a conduit and should be able to freely let go of the physical instruments because you cannot lose its eternal affluence. With this settled, you can learn the skills and wisdom of handling wealth and God's blessings on the earth and look forward to receiving a greater measure in eternity because your works, says the Lord, do follow you. The secret is to keep mammon as your slave and to be determined to leave the planet richer toward God than this world, as the Lord Jesus teaches in Luke 12:21; "So is he that layeth up treasure for himself, and is not rich toward God."

After paper chasing for years, I finally heard the Lord's voice concerning money and my idea of acquiring it. Having grown almost ritualistic in my prayers for it, I began to hear the Lord say, "you have money." In disbelief, I countered Him with where and how, because I knew what my bankbook said. I knew my debts and the barriers I faced in relieving them. I had the facts and they said I did not have money, certainly not the money I needed. God spoke again. "You have more money than you know what to do with; you will not spend all the wealth I have given you in ten lifetimes and your seed to the fourth generation cannot exhaust it." I was mystified as to what He was talking about because in my mind cash equaled money and I did not have much of that; for sure, I did not have the amount He said I possessed. "Where is it?" I asked. "How do I get it? If this is true, why am I broke?" Sound familiar? I would love to tell you that I got it right away and life turn around and was rosy. I did not and it did not. There was more to learn and understand. My early money classes had trained me well through ridiculous losses, lack on all sides, and setbacks that came straight out of the surreal. I am sure you know what I am talking about and can bear witness to what mental state I was in when the Lord said I had all this money.

Out of respect for God, I tried not to argue and even forced myself to pretend that I believed what He said; although, at the time, I was unable to do so. I got very religious, quoted the scriptures I knew, and just dropped the matter. I simply did not know what to do with His words and could not fathom how the vast wealth He stated I had, would ever come my way. It was easier to just feel like He meant that something spiritual would take place when I went to heaven. However, for now, I had reality to face and

42

that meant I needed to resume my quest for the cash to pay my bills. You know the thought line. I needn't drag it out.

Still somehow, things did not get better, and my prayers remained the same. When the pressure mounted, God responded with the same statement. Over time, it got old and frustrating, but we know that the Lord cannot change and cannot lie. So, because He maintained that I had all this money, I finally felt the urge to find out how and where. That took more time, but as you can see this book is evidence of what I learned. He began my class with "Money is a spirit because I created it and I am Spirit." I knew that, but I resolved to keep silent and to go along with what He was showing me at the pace He wanted me to learn. Here is an example that helped me get it. Suppose you have been out of work for more than six months. Your bills are piled high, your phone rings incessantly and you know that it's your creditors. You hit the pavement daily to get a job and finally you succeed. You get a promise to start in two weeks and the salary is beyond your expectations.

Suddenly, even though you have yet to get a paycheck, your mood changes and your attitude changes. Why? Because you have a job, the first valuable thing to come to you after your promise of employment is *hope*—that's a value and a high kingdom currency. When your hope is gone, you can bet you will not have any wealth, no matter how much cash you have on hand. Even if you are wealthy, once you become spiritually destitute you may as well be dirt poor. To continue, confidence joins hope and if you are given to rashness, maybe even a little cockiness, you begin to feel you can take those calls you were dodging and give your creditors the good news. You can resume payments and even make some payment arrangements even though you still have no money.

The company that hired you has the money and you have a promise, another prized kingdom currency, and for you (and strangely your creditors) for now, those are good enough. But why is that the case? What is it that made them think things are going to be all right with you now that made you feel as if you can take on life again? The answer is *words*. The words, "we want you to start on such-and-such date" lifted your spirits and ignited your *hope*. Your *confidence* in the company and its commitment to its word were as good as money in the bank to you because you know that once you are on the payroll that *promise*, when it is transformed, becomes money in the bank. Jesus states in John 6:63 that words are spirit, and as such, they bring life. So important is the *spirit* of things that the Bible tells us that the (human) body without it is dead (see James 2:26). Such a principle carries over to your economic existence. Once a word is spoken, invisible spiritual workers go to work to see that they stay alive and formulate until they bring the sound into a physical body or substance that can be handled by you.

The hiring officer's words released the spirit of life in you again and you believed the words that your new employer was going to pay you for your qualifications. They took the initiative to demonstrate their *faith* in you. You responded in kind by acting on their faith and allowing your own to come alive in your life. They trust that what you say you can do and what you showed them in the interview process is worth the dollar amount they agreed to pay you. You trust that two weeks from today according to their word you will work for pay and a week or so after that you will get a literal paycheck and begin to reverse the fortunes of your life.

Do you notice anything peculiar about this scenario? As yet, no cash has changed hands and still you are able to get some things on credit, perhaps borrow money against your paycheck and overall cease to feel broke or poor. Nothing on the surface has changed and yet the exchange of words, promises, and an offer constitute money for you. The reason is because *money is a spirit and the cash you now wait for is its body.* The cash from your anticipated paycheck, treated as already in hand, is merely an instrument that will attest to your personal and professional worth to an organization. Its willingness to agree with your self-valuation enough to open its treasury for you is the real money. That check is just a monetary note on your ability to enrich your company. It is that for which you are being rewarded, but remember, it all started with what is inside you. Before you ever get a withdrawal from their treasury you cashed in on your own. You opened the hiring agent's heart to you and that led to the job offer that opened the company's treasury and added to your personal economy. Your self worth was sold as economically worthwhile to them. It is the same with the Lord.

The things that make for money are not what make for wealth. That comes from entirely different spiritual forces, as money is the means by which wealth is obtained. Take away the exchange aspect of the process and you have cash and cash alone. If you do not spend, exchange, invest, or otherwise transform your cash into wealth, sooner or later you will be broke again. At the least, you will just know the potential of wealth and never experience its satisfaction. You

45

have security but little stability. Cash can be lost or stolen and not invested and it will not increase. It remains dollar for dollar, which is why the Lord rebuked the servant that hid His talent in the ground. He wanted each servant to understand the law of increase by depositing His money with the bankers so that at least He could get interest on His money. Creation works on increase, a strange truth, because money is a spirit. What makes wealth then, you ask? *You do,* and that is the highest and most veiled secret of money; it is the secret that its godless world administrators want to keep hidden from you.

Chapter Seven
Cashing in on You

Money, more precisely wealth, is you, and you are wealth. The moment you begin to see yourself and what you produce from yourself as valuable and garner the confidence you need to convince others who have the cash to pay for it, you will cease to lack money. Your challenge will then be how to increase and sustain what you are now making. You are your own wealth center. Your know-how, your experience, your abilities and skills, your talent and instincts are all wealth generators. You turn them on by believing, expressing them to others, exerting effort (work), and honing them to the point of being trade worthy.

As a matter of fact, one of the six or so words for money, wealth, or riches in the Old Testament is a strange word called *hown*. It is pronounced "hone" and one of its many meanings is that of a self-made person whose wealth and riches come as a result of his or her own efforts. It carries with it the connotation of one who brought forth into view the riches and wealth hidden or stored within, presenting the idea of *exnihilo*, a something-from-nothing wealth (see Ecclesiastes 6:2; Proverbs 13:11 and 10:15). Nothing says better than this explanation that money is a spirit, and as a spirit God's first begotten offspring, Jesus Christ, has full authority over it. Refer to Matthew 28:18. The question is not whether you ever have money at your disposal. The real issue is whether or not you are willing to do what it takes to bring it outside of yourself and into your world. Can you

47

believe in your God given talents enough to awaken the powerful prosperity that is right now asleep inside you? It's a tough call, and you need to know that in the beginning you are going to be in for a fight because you are awakening and engaging a formidable giant. This giant has ruled you and your thinking for some time. Rooted in scripture, this reality has asserted itself time and again. Mammon perceives itself a god and you its slave, or at the least its pawn. It takes greater power than it has wielded in your life for years to overturn this mindset and to dethrone its position.

For instance, the word most commonly used for money in the Old Testament is the word *chayil*. It first shows up in Deuteronomy 8:17-18 where Yahweh admonishes Israel against taking credit for the enormous wealth He was about to release to His covenant people. The passage says that it is the Lord who gives *power* to get wealth as a testimonial of His covenant with His people. That statement is replete with implications. Do you have a covenant with Him through His Son Jesus Christ? If you do, then expect the same power to be at your disposal. *Chayil* speaks to a powerful person able to engage and plunder an enemy in order to possess his or her goods. The spirit of the word and its applications is behind the Lord Jesus' parable of the strongman in Matthew 12:29. Warfare figures into wealth-getting because it is presumed that a stronger person, one who will fight you rather than surrender it to you, holds it.

Romans 5:2 introduces the idea of our having a special access to the Lord and the beneficial blessings of His Spirit. Following up on this idea is Ephesians 2:18 that says now Gentiles can be fellow heirs and partakers of Israel's commonwealth; the same commonwealth that the Lord presented to His people ages ago in Deuteronomy 8:17-18.

Later in Ephesians 3:10-15, Paul offers up a poignant prayer to the Father concerning our relationship with Him and His Son. First of all, he prays that the powers and principalities in the heavenly places (the same Old Testament high places) might comprehend Creator God's manifold wisdom through its witness of His eternal purpose unfolded in and by the church of Jesus Christ on earth. Now what else does that speak to except that money and everything earthly has a spiritual lineage and prototype? From here, Paul seeks that we understand the boldness that we are given in Jesus Christ; a boldness that empowers us to access (that is, gain admission to) all that those who are named in the family of God in heaven and earth have the right of enter. Those who descend from God the Father through the Lord Jesus Christ have this special access to whatever and all that our spiritual relatives access. Here is what Revelation 19:10 means when the angel that spoke with John admonished him not to worship him, seeing as he was a fellow servant and brother. How can an angel claim kinship with humans? In the Lord Jesus Christ, that's how. The angel being named after Jesus, as we are, recognized the special family relationship God created between His heavenly and earthly family.

The point of this discussion is that you must learn to touch hearts to open their treasuries because the Savior told us that where people's treasures are their hearts would also be. Succinctly speaking, hearts follow the treasure, and unfortunately for far too many people, treasure drives the heart. However unpleasant the idea may be, there are very

49

good people who love the Lord and are entrusted with His wealth. In Genesis, Melchizedek was one such person who paved the way for Abraham's covenantal blessings from the Almighty. Abraham, after receiving the spiritual blessings of the Creator's priest on earth, goes on to become wealthy enough to gain the recognition and respect of surrounding monarchs. God's favor brought him before kings (see Proverbs 22:29).

Following suit, Abraham's sons, because of his standing with the Most High, inherit their wealth and so it goes down the line. Genesis chapter 28 recounts an incident where Jacob saw heaven's gate or portal and the Lord's angels ascending and descending upon a ladder. This vision precipitated the appearance of the Lord God, who reinstituted Abraham's covenant with his son as He had promised. The incident turned out to be the spiritual bestowal of wealth and prominence that exists in the planet today. Not unlike Abraham's covenantal blessings earlier in the text, Jacob was to father the twelve patriarchs who would eventually become the twelve tribes of Israel, Jacob's divine name. The man's wealth was released from heaven in the form of a promise, a promise that he believed. It was necessary for this to happen since his father and grandfather were dead. To prove the wealth that was injected into Abraham's seed traveled down the line to succeeding generations, the Lord of the covenant appeared to Jacob, as He had done with the others, to assure them that what began with their father did not end at his demise; it merely passed along to the next eligible heir.

The value of the reference to our teaching is that before the wealth of the Lord passed on to Jacob, who fled and no doubt took little with him to survive on, it had to be interjected into the earth by way of his forefathers' hearing hearts. Believing the vision, something that was not as difficult back then as it is today, Jacob proceeded with the call of the Lord on his life and became powerful.

Centuries later, the Lord Jesus, as the divine sire of the New Creation, draws the words of Jacob forward for the Son of Man. To let us know that what was done under the old covenant was still active in the earth and that His provisions were already delivered into the planet to service His ministry, Jesus uses the same phrase to explain how and why He would be successful (see John 1:51 that corresponds with Genesis 28:12). In the passage, He answers Nathaniel's faith remark. Jesus says that because of his faith he would be privy to the means by which the Messiah would be provided for in the earth. Nathaniel would see the heavens open and the angels of God ascending and descending, this time not upon a ladder or heavenly staircase, but upon the Son of Man (notice He chose Son of Man over Son of God). What could that mean but what it meant centuries earlier to Jacob, and no doubt Abraham? The Lord Himself had descended and brought with Him the fullness of heaven's blessings. The very fact that He entered the planet indicates an uninterrupted flow of spiritual blessings to manifest in our material world. Later when the Holy Spirit came, the deal was sealed and the blessings of eternity were deposited in the earth in a measure exceeding the power of the material possession of the previous covenant confined to this world.

Now under the Christ covenant—the Messianic covenant—it is *"every spiritual blessing in the heavenly places,"* as Ephesians 1:3 and 1:20 say. Heavenly places means above the sky in the sphere of the celestial rather than terrestrial. Ephesians 2:6 says how and why we now have access to them. We have been raised up and made to sit together with Christ Jesus in those heavenly places. That is one reason why when you intensely pray for money or financial turnarounds you see it in the form of visions and dreams, as though they already exist and are merely awaiting your possession. Ephesians 2:7 adds God's purpose (eternal purpose) is that in the ages to come the Lord might show the exceeding riches of His grace to His children in and through Jesus Christ. This is not only speaking to futuristic spiritual riches; but apparently, from what we see in the world today among the family of God, it includes this world's material riches in whatever measure the Lord God has assigned to us.

Chapter Eight
God Programmed You to
Prosper & Profit

By now the point is nearly made, but there are yet more details to establish you in the dynamics of the spirits of wealth, money, and mammon. Since all things begin in the spirit and find their express manifestations in the flesh, it behooves you to grow rich in the spirit to possess your wealth in the natural. That means for you who belong to the Lord Jesus Christ, the Lord of all wealth, you must grow rich in God; otherwise, your riches will fly away when you least expect, or your heirs will be impoverished when you depart the planet. Here is what the Savior alludes to as a consequence of not seeking first God's kingdom and its righteousness. Here is what Luke 12:21 wants us to accept about spiritual wealth. He who is consumed with only the riches of this world ultimately fails God: "So is he that layeth up treasure for himself, and is not rich toward God."

To tie this all together, take yourself for an example. God literally built you to prosper and profit. More specifically, He constructed you with power to get wealth. He then founded the world in such a way that you would have ample opportunity to do so.

God chose parents, situations, circumstances, and a host of other well thought-out factors to provoke you to dig deep inside yourself and pull up what He already ordained for you to produce wealth. Knowledge has long been accepted as a source of wealth, and as I have shown, so has wisdom. Skills, understanding, and insight are all branches of knowledge that serve our purposes to this end. Emotions are another thought of wealth; at least, they provide you with potential wealth access. Your likes, dislikes, tastes, and such are all part of the portfolio of wealth potential the Lord gave you free of charge, which is why they fall under the category of inheritance. All you had to do to get them is to be born. What you think of as your negative traits are so because they bring you no profit, nor can you see anyway anyone could appreciate them. This is especially so if you have been belittled or scorned for being who you are or doing things the way you cannot help but do them. Therefore, they cost you and seem to bring you only pain. While they tend to increase after their own kind, some (almost all) personality traits, idiosyncrasies, or drives have a goal that is only unprofitable when they yield only detrimental and disastrous results. However, when you see yourself as a wealth center (potentially or not), what may be negative sides of your personality or personhood can well be turned into profitability.

Take for instance some people's habit of finding fault in everything. In social and relational settings, this can be vexing, but in a professional context, it can be profitable. This is because critics are those people who detect inferiority, shortfalls, and possible danger. Are you one who cannot keep a secret and always tell people's business, almost without thinking about it? One way to control that is to divert it to communicating something people need and cannot easily get. Enter the field of journalism or public speaking. Your perfectly good gift could then be wisely applied.

How about those of you who just can't stay home and hate being alone? Perhaps you are called to hospitality, where you can profit from your need to be around people and socialize. Are you one who loves to start projects and then move on to the next thing? Maybe God endowed you to be a project manager or events sponsor. Or take the one who slows every process down to get it just right, or who will find the one thing wrong in an apparently excellent venture or project, and you will find a quality control/assurance person. The helpless clean freak, the one who loves to argue or debate, the reckless athlete, or even the one who loves too much peace and quiet all exhibit natural inclinations deliberately bestowed in support of a profitable endeavor or career.

Today's wide open arena has shown us that there is a profitable place for you, if you seek to connect what you hate about yourself with someone's else's need or delight. Try seeing what you do to irritate people or what comes far too easy for you to do with what others would appreciate — your natural abilities, raw or not. What is fun, easy, and almost compulsive to you may be what the Creator endowed you with to prosper. It becomes clear, in this light, to see how cash and dollars were never your problem. Faith, direction, training, and determination are the real lack. They, without a talent or a talent without an outlet, create lack. Your riches are in you, and when you see richness and wealth through the eyes of the Creator, you get an entirely different picture of what it takes for you to gain your spiritual inheritance. By spiritual, I mean that Creator endowed abundance that only you and what you are made of can profitably attract or embody in your life.

Strong's #4147 is one Greek word for *rich* as used in scripture. It is the word *plouteo*, pronounced *ploo-teh'-o*. It means "to be or become wealthy in every sphere of existence, spiritually and naturally." The manner is simple: by being increased with goods. "To be enriched to the point of being made wealthy, endowed or bestowed riches, possessions, money, and valuables in abundance." These are all a result of being filled to the full or fulfilling what one has been blessed by God to accomplish, achieve, supply, or furnish in return for spiritual, financial, or another type of comparable remuneration.

On your own time, look up the Bible's references for *riches* and *prosperity* as well as *profit* and *profitable*. Also, if you want to get your life and lifestyle on the road to the Lord's riches, wealth, and prosperity, study the following scriptures. Do **not** study these for theological content or spiritual consolation; but rather for the insight and guidance they give you on how to alter your existence to access and retrieve your New Creation inheritance from the Lord's divine treasury.

For further enlightenment on *inheritance* in the New Creation, see Acts 20:32, where the word *kleronomia* is used. It defines a possession, specifically one that is inherited. It is used in Acts 26:18, where *kleros* represents a die (dice) for drawing chances. The Bible explains this as casting lots; it is a predetermined portion distributed to a person's *lot* in life before they are born. It further pertains to an acquisition, heritage, and inheritance. Galatians 3:18 adds *kleronomia* to define heirship and the possession one acquires as an inheritance. Ephesians 1:11 further includes in our explanation the New Testament word *kleroo*, which means, "to allot to one as an assigned privilege." Collectively, these terms tell us how and why wealth is a spirit and is distributed according to divine administrative guidelines. They are part of every human being's Creator bestowed possessions, and as His creatures, are not earned or seized but acquired as part of an inheritance. The measures and distributions are determined by lots, under the direction of unseen hands, charged by God with the distribution of His eternal fortunes. The fortunes, as we come to know them, were allotted before time began, as Psalm 139:15-18 seems to imply, based on what the Lord assigned us to do in this world, and thus included various privileges associated with wealth, stature, and prestige gained in this world.

As you can see, these words are not merely futuristic trusts set up for us in eternity once we leave the earth. They include right now privileges, bequests left by Jesus Christ to His body, as well as portions of what He inherited from the Father to be enjoyed by Himself and His body. They are inherited by the new birth by those born again into the very nativity of our Savior and by the divine right bestowed upon Him as the Son of God.

Spiritually, God's idea of wealth, particularly what occurs from being made wealthy as a consequence of becoming rich toward Him, carries with it the idea of being *imbued*, saturated with wealth diffusing and attracting properties that permeate one's being. Here is what God means when He says He gives us **power to get wealth**. What Christ imparted to you at redemption, He transferred to you by placing you into His kingdom of wealth. The idea of biblical wealth is the inborn possession of an influence that supersedes what is normal for most people in your class, position, or status. It indicates a wealth generating potential where all you do and touch is made to prosper as if of its own accord. What the Lord has supplied to you before you were born is released under His prescribed circumstance to see that your spiritual blessings supply your natural provisions in abundance. What would you say is a good example of spiritual goods that would constitute one's richness toward God? What do you presently possess, and perhaps are dismissing as insignificant, that God placed in you to be your conduit of wealth? Your answer to these two questions begins your admittance into your spiritual treasury to release it to create your natural wealth stream.

To begin though, you are going to have to change your views and attitudes about mammon and money. They are not evil in and of themselves; it is people's means of acquiring and distributing them that makes them appear so. If you desire to bless the Lord and His kingdom, then you will need an abundance of both to get the job done. If, on the other hand, your heart is according to James 4:1-3, then it may be the Lord's reasons for holding back your normally deserved wealth streams. God is not interested in your world acclaim, your power, or your influence in the world and sphere of humanity. He is interested in one thing and one thing only: saving souls. In doing so, the Father succeeds in manifesting His Son's kingdom. With all the Lord gives us to do, He aims to glorify Jesus and His work on the cross. God seeks to get His Spirit into as many souls as possible, and get His New Creation church from here to eternity. If you are sincere, diligent, and determined to take up the task of helping Him do this, then by His Spirit you will be provided for above and beyond your need—more than you will ever ask, think, or use— because *money is a spirit.*

Chapter Nine
How to Start

Now that you are at the place of understanding the spirit of money and your New Creation embodiment of its potential and properties, you are well on your way to breaking free to alter your financial position from the inside out. Still, it is one thing to have read this book and agree with its principles, and it is another thing to actually open the door to wealth building. There is still more to do. You must begin to put all you have learned to work, starting with a review of the nine points discussed in chapter two. Evaluate yourself to see where you stand with them.

Next you want to go back over your life and assess your treatment of people and the tasks you were assigned. Many people, especially younger ones, feel the end justifies the means, and for a short while, it may seem to be true. However, just as good will has profitability and worth, so does ill will. Leaving a long trail of unfinished business, incomplete projects, and hurt and mistreated people adds up. As hard as it is to believe, people's emotions intensify and too many bad reports from others will backfire on you in the end. At a time when you least expect it, those murmurings and angry voices will be heard, and when they are, all the hearts you have closed will cost you. Proverbs says that people are valued by what others say about them.

Here are some more considerations as you work on your wealth manifesting attitudes. Do you believe it when Proverbs says the hand of the diligent will prosper? If you do, how would you rate your diligence in action? What about sowing and reaping? Have you jumped ship on your harvest season? How about your service and sacrifice mentality? Are you attached to a place where you can serve, and while doing so, derive the benefits of increased skill, wisdom, and opportunities? Go through the list yourself and rate your readiness for moving into this new realm.

What about your prayer life, your interactions with the very God that you expect to release your wealth? When He does, how prepared are you to use it wisely and remain devoted to Him? Will your newfound wealth and success be the reasons you give Him for abandoning your work in His church, finding time to pray, or fulfilling responsibilities you had before you "arrived," so to speak? Are you one of those who want to be home promptly at five with dinner at six and the news at nine? Are you able to make adjustments to do what it takes to increase your wealth, including increased effort and taking on a greater workload if need be, or are you set on getting the most for the least? Do you feel you have to have it all now already and are just demanding God to make you rich quick? If you do, you are vulnerable to predators, charlatans, and con artists who will exploit your impatience and greed. How about planning? Are you in a hurry to just get started and decide to figure things out along the way, or can you let wisdom guide your planning and implementation processes?

There is also the matter of your social relationships and networking skills. Far too many people are devoted to being islands intent on showing the world they made it by themselves and did not have to rely on or work with anyone. If this is you, rethink that belief. Whatever God calls you to do, He means for it to be part of some whole He already has

61

working. Generally speaking, no matter how new your venture may be to you, the Lord has had something working in that area before you to lay the foundation. Others paved the way and set up circumstances for what you will add to the venture. Do not become too bent on being a lone ranger. God wants His family to operate as one, and that means you should be on the lookout for those He selected to work with you, either as a mentor or partner.

In relation to your vision, do your homework. Learn about the others in your area who are working on similar projects and collaborate with them on your vision. Partner with or *serve* those doing what you want to do, ideally before you begin your project, to get their wisdom. In addition, study your subject thoroughly and do not be afraid to take a class on it; it can only help.

So far we have discussed your position in the nine-point list for breaking the seal on money's wisdom, your present belief system, and attitudes you may have for getting where you want to be, and what you are willing to do to comply with money's laws of acquisition and accumulation.

In conclusion, I recommend you study Proverbs, God's wisdom book. Proverbs 16:3 instruct us to commit our works to the Lord and He will establish our thoughts concerning them. To balance it all out, Proverbs 16:8 warns us to choose righteousness and right, even over great revenues. These two pieces of information serve as valuable guidelines for keeping wealth, as well as your pursuit of it in godly perspective.

Appendix
Your Wealth Study Guide:
Wealth Scriptures for You to Study

Study these on your own to get God's mind and motives for your never having a money problem again.

1. Genesis 34:29 KJV: And all their **wealth**, and all their little ones, and their wives took they captive, and spoiled even all that was in the house.
2. Deuteronomy 8:17 KJV: And thou say in thine heart, my power and the might of mine hand hath gotten me this **wealth**.
3. Deuteronomy 8:18 KJV: But thou shalt remember the LORD thy God: for it is he that giveth thee power to get **wealth**, that he may establish his covenant which he sware unto thy fathers, as it is this day.
4. Ruth 2:1 KJV: And Naomi had a kinsman of her husband's, a mighty man of **wealth**, of the family of Elimelech; and his name was Boaz.
5. 1 Samuel 2:32 KJV: And thou shalt see an enemy in my habitation, in all the **wealth** which God shall give Israel: and there shall not be an old man in thine house for ever.
6. 2 Kings 15:20 KJV: And Menahem exacted the money of Israel, even of all the mighty men of **wealth**, of each man

fifty shekels of silver, to give to the king of Assyria. So the king of Assyria turned back, and stayed not there in the land.

7. 2 Chronicles 1:11 KJV: And God said to Solomon, "Because this was in thine heart, and thou hast not asked riches, **wealth**, or honour, nor the life of thine enemies, neither yet hast asked long life; but hast asked wisdom and knowledge for thyself, that thou mayest judge my people, over whom I have made thee king."

8. 2 Chronicles 1:12 KJV: Wisdom and knowledge is granted unto thee; and I will give thee riches, and **wealth**, and honour, such as none of the kings have had that have been before thee; neither shall there any after thee have the like.

9. Ezra 9:12 KJV: Now therefore give not your daughters unto their sons, neither take their daughters unto your sons, nor seek their peace or their **wealth** for ever: that ye may be strong, and eat the good of the land, and leave it for an inheritance to your children for ever.

10. Esther 10:3 KJV: For Mordecai the Jew was next unto king Ahasuerus, and great among the Jews, and accepted of the multitude of his brethren, seeking the **wealth** of his people, and speaking peace to all his seed.

11. Job 21:13 KJV: They spend their days in **wealth**, and in a moment go down to the grave.

12. Job 31:25 KJV: If I rejoiced because my **wealth** was great, and because mine hand had gotten much;

13. Psalm 44:12 KJV: Thou sellest thy people for nought, and dost not increase thy **wealth** by their price.

14. Psalm 49:6 KJV: They that trust in their **wealth**, and boast themselves in the multitude of their riches

15. Psalm 49:10 KJV: For he seeth that wise men die, likewise the fool and the brutish person perish, and leave their **wealth** to others.

16. Psalm 112:3 KJV: **Wealth** and riches shall be in his house: and his righteousness endureth for ever.

17. Proverbs 5:10 KJV: Lest strangers be filled with thy **wealth**; and thy labours be in the house of a stranger

18. Proverbs 10:15 KJV: The rich man's **wealth** is his strong city: the destruction of the poor is their poverty.

19. Proverbs 13:11 KJV: **Wealth** gotten by vanity shall be diminished: but he that gathereth by labour shall increase.

20. Proverbs 13:22 KJV: A good man leaveth an inheritance to his children's children: and the **wealth** of the sinner is laid up

for the just.

21. Proverbs 18:11 KJV: The rich man's **wealth** is his strong city, and as a high wall in his own conceit.

22. Proverbs 19:4 KJV: **Wealth** maketh many friends; but the poor is separated from his neighbour.

23. Ecclesiastes 5:19 KJV: Every man also to whom God hath given riches and **wealth**, and hath given him power to eat thereof, and to take his portion, and to rejoice in his labour; this is the gift of God.

24. Ecclesiastes 6:2 KJV: A man to whom God hath given riches, **wealth**, and honour, so that he wanteth nothing for his soul of all that he desireth, yet God giveth him not power to eat thereof, but a stranger eateth it: this is vanity, and it is an evil disease.

25. Zechariah 14:14 KJV: And Judah also shall fight at Jerusalem; and the **wealth** of all the heathen round about shall be gathered together, gold, and silver, and apparel, in great abundance.

26. Acts 19:25 KJV: Whom he called together with the workmen of like occupation, and said, "Sirs, ye know that by this craft we have our **wealth**."

27. 1 Corinthians 10:24 KJV: Let no man seek his own, but every man another's

wealth.

Money Passages of Scripture

1. Genesis 17:12 KJV: And he that is eight days old shall be circumcised among you, every man child in your generations, he that is born in the house, or bought with **money** of any stranger, which is not of thy seed.
2. Genesis 17:13 KJV: He that is born in thy house, and he that is bought with thy **money**, must needs be circumcised: and my covenant shall be in your flesh for an everlasting covenant.
3. Genesis 17:23 KJV: And Abraham took Ishmael his son, and all that were born in his house, and all that were bought with his **money**, every male among the men of Abraham's house; and circumcised the flesh of their foreskin in the selfsame day, as God had said unto him.
4. Genesis 17:27 KJV: And all the men of his house, born in the house, and bought with **money** of the stranger, were circumcised with him.
5. Genesis 23:9 KJV: That he may give me the cave of Machpelah, which he hath, which is in the end of his field; for as much **money** as it is worth he shall give it me for a possession of a burying place

amongst you.

6. Genesis 23:13 KJV: - And he spake unto Ephron in the audience of the people of the land, saying, "But if thou wilt give it, I pray thee, hear me: I will give thee **money** for the field; take it of me, and I will bury my dead there."

7. Genesis 23:16 KJV: And Abraham hearkened unto Ephron; and Abraham weighed to Ephron the silver, which he had named in the audience of the sons of Heth, four hundred shekels of silver, current **money** with the merchant.

8. Genesis 31:15 KJV: Are we not counted of him strangers? For he hath sold us, and hath quite devoured also our **money**.

9. Genesis 33:19 KJV: And he bought a parcel of a field, where he had spread his tent, at the hand of the children of Hamor, Shechem's father, for an hundred pieces of **money**.

10. Genesis 42:25 KJV: Then Joseph commanded to fill their sacks with corn, and to restore every man's **money** into his sack, and to give them provision for the way: and thus did he unto them.

11. Genesis 42:27 KJV: And as one of them opened his sack to give his ass provender in the inn, he espied his **money**; for, behold, it was in his sack's

mouth.

12. Genesis 42:28 KJV: And he said unto his brethren, "My **money** is restored; and, lo, it is even in my sack;" and their heart failed them, and they were afraid, saying one to another, "What is this that God hath done unto us?"

13. Genesis 42:35 KJV: And it came to pass as they emptied their sacks, that, behold, every man's bundle of **money** was in his sack: and when both they and their father saw the bundles of money, they were afraid.

14. Genesis 43:12 KJV: And take double money in your hand; and the **money** that was brought again in the mouth of your sacks, carry it again in your hand; peradventure it was an oversight

15. Genesis 43:15 KJV: And the men took that present, and they took double **money** in their hand, and Benjamin; and rose up, and went down to Egypt, and stood before Joseph.

16. Genesis 43:18 KJV: And the men were afraid, because they were brought into Joseph's house; and they said, "Because of the **money** that was returned in our sacks at the first time are we brought in; that he may seek occasion against us, and fall upon us, and take us for bondmen, and our asses."

17. Genesis 43:21 KJV: And it came to pass, when we came to the inn, that we opened our sacks, and, behold, every man's **money** was in the mouth of his sack, our money in full weight: and we have brought it again in our hand.

18. Genesis 43:22 KJV: And other **money** have we brought down in our hands to buy food: we cannot tell who put our **money** in our sacks.

19. Genesis 43:23 KJV: And he said, "Peace be to you, fear not: your God, and the God of your father, hath given you treasure in your sacks: I had your **money**." And he brought Simeon out unto them.

20. Genesis 44:1 KJV: And he commanded the steward of his house, saying, Fill the men's sacks with food, as much as they can carry, and put every man's **money** in his sack's mouth.

21. Genesis 44:2 KJV: And put my cup, the silver cup, in the sack's mouth of the youngest, and his corn **money**. And he did according to the word that Joseph had spoken.

22. Genesis 44:8 KJV: Behold, the **money**, which we found in our sacks' mouths, we brought again unto thee out of the land of Canaan: how then should we steal out of thy lord's house silver or

gold?

23. Genesis 47:14 KJV: And Joseph gathered up all the **money** that was found in the land of Egypt, and in the land of Canaan, for the corn which they bought: and Joseph brought the **money** into Pharaoh's house.

24. Genesis 47:15 KJV: And when **money** failed in the land of Egypt, and in the land of Canaan, all the Egyptians came unto Joseph, and said, "Give us bread: for why should we die in thy presence? For the **money** faileth."

25. Genesis 47:16 KJV: And Joseph said, "Give your cattle; and I will give you for your cattle, if **money** fail."

26. Genesis 47:18 KJV: When that year was ended, they came unto him the second year, and said unto him, "We will not hide it from my lord, how that our **money** is spent; my lord also hath our herds of cattle; there is not ought left in the sight of my lord, but our bodies, and our lands."

27. Exodus 12:44 KJV: But every man's servant that is bought for **money**, when thou hast circumcised him, then shall he eat thereof.

28. Exodus 21:11 KJV: And if he do not these three unto her, then shall she go out free without **money**.

29. Exodus 21:21 KJV: Notwithstanding, if he continue a day or two, he shall not be punished: for he is his **money**.

30. Exodus 21:30 KJV: If there be laid on him a sum of money, then he shall give for the ransom of his life whatsoever is laid upon him.

31. Exodus 21:34 KJV: The owner of the pit shall make it good, and give **money** unto the owner of them; and the dead beast shall be his.

32. Exodus 21:35 KJV: And if one man's ox hurt another's that he die; then they shall sell the live ox, and divide the **money** of it; and the dead ox also they shall divide.

33. Exodus 22:7 KJV: If a man shall deliver unto his neighbour **money** or stuff to keep, and it be stolen out of the man's house; if the thief be found, let him pay double.

34. Exodus 22:17 KJV: If her father utterly refuse to give her unto him, he shall pay **money** according to the dowry of virgins.

35. Exodus 22:25 KJV: If thou lend **money** to any of my people that is poor by thee, thou shalt not be to him as an usurer, neither shalt thou lay upon him usury.

36. Exodus 30:16 KJV: And thou shalt take the atonement **money** of the children of

Israel, and shalt appoint it for the service of the tabernacle of the congregation; that it may be a memorial unto the children of Israel before the LORD, to make an atonement for your souls.

37. Leviticus 22:11 KJV: But if the priest buy any soul with his **money**, he shall eat of it, and he that is born in his house: they shall eat of his meat.

38. Leviticus 25:37 KJV: Thou shalt not give him thy **money** upon usury, nor lend him thy victuals for increase.

39. Leviticus 25:51 KJV: If there be yet many years behind, according unto them he shall give again the price of his redemption out of the **money** that he was bought for.

40. Leviticus 27:15 KJV: And if he that sanctified it will redeem his house, then he shall add the fifth part of the **money** of thy estimation unto it, and it shall be his.

41. Leviticus 27:18 KJV: But if he sanctify his field after the jubilee, then the priest shall reckon unto him the **money** according to the years that remain, even unto the year of the jubilee, and it shall be abated from thy estimation.

42. Leviticus 27:19 KJV: And if he that sanctified the field will in any wise

redeem it, then he shall add the fifth part of the **money** of thy estimation unto it, and it shall be assured to him.

43. Numbers 3:48 KJV): And thou shalt give the **money**, wherewith the odd number of them is to be redeemed, unto Aaron and to his sons.

44. Numbers 3:49 KJV: And Moses took the redemption **money** of them that were over and above them that were redeemed by the Levites.

45. Numbers 3:50 KJV: Of the firstborn of the children of Israel took he the **money**; a thousand three hundred and threescore and five shekels, after the shekel of the sanctuary:

46. Numbers 3:51 KJV: And Moses gave the **money** of them that were redeemed unto Aaron and to his sons, according to the word of the LORD, as the LORD commanded Moses.

47. Numbers 18:16 KJV: And those that are to be redeemed from a month old shalt thou redeem, according to thine estimation, for the **money** of five shekels, after the shekel of the sanctuary, which is twenty *gerahs*.

48. Deuteronomy 2:6 KJV: Ye shall buy meat of them for **money**, that ye may eat; and ye shall also buy water of them for money, that ye may drink.

74

49. Deuteronomy 2:28 KJV: Thou shalt sell me meat for **money**, that I may eat; and give me water for money, that I may drink: only I will pass through on my feet.

50. Deuteronomy 14:25 KJV: Then shalt thou turn it into **money**, and bind up the money in thine hand, and shalt go unto the place which the LORD thy God shall choose.

51. Deuteronomy 14:26 KJV: And thou shalt bestow that **money** for whatsoever thy soul lusteth after, for oxen, or for sheep, or for wine, or for strong drink, or for whatsoever thy soul desireth: and thou shalt eat there before the LORD thy God, and thou shalt rejoice, thou, and thine household,

52. Deuteronomy 21:14 KJV: And it shall be, if thou have no delight in her, then thou shalt let her go whither she will; but thou shalt not sell her at all for **money**, thou shalt not make merchandise of her, because thou hast humbled her.

53. Deuteronomy 23:19 KJV: Thou shalt not lend upon usury to thy brother; usury of **money**, usury of victuals, usury of any thing that is lent upon usury.

54. Judges 5:19 KJV: The kings came and fought, then fought the kings of Canaan

in Taanach by the waters of Megiddo; they took no gain of **money**.

55. Judges 16:18 KJV: And when Delilah saw that he had told her all his heart, she sent and called for the lords of the Philistines, saying, "Come up this once, for he hath showed me all his heart." Then the lords of the Philistines came up unto her, and brought **money** in their hand.

56. Judges 17:4 KJV: Yet he restored the **money** unto his mother; and his mother took two hundred shekels of silver, and gave them to the founder, who made thereof a graven image and a molten image: and they were in the house of Micah.

57. 1 Kings 21:2 KJV: And Ahab spake unto Naboth, saying, "Give me thy vineyard, that I may have it for a garden of herbs, because it is near unto my house: and I will give thee for it a better vineyard than it; or, if it seem good to thee, I will give thee the worth of it in **money**."

58. 1 Kings 21:6 KJV: And he said unto her, "Because I spake unto Naboth the Jezreelite, and said unto him, 'Give me thy vineyard for **money**; or else, if it please thee, I will give thee another vineyard for it;' and he answered, 'I will not give thee my vineyard.'

59. 1 Kings 21:15 KJV: And it came to pass, when Jezebel heard that Naboth was stoned, and was dead, that Jezebel said to Ahab, "Arise, take possession of the vineyard of Naboth the Jezreelite, which he refused to give thee for **money**: for Naboth is not alive, but dead."

60. 2 Kings 5:26 KJV: And he said unto him, "Went not mine heart with thee, when the man turned again from his chariot to meet thee? Is it a time to receive **money**, and to receive garments, and oliveyards, and vineyards, and sheep, and oxen, and menservants, and maidservants?"

61. 2 Kings 12:4 KJV: And Jehoash said to the priests, "All the **money** of the dedicated things that is brought into the house of the LORD, even the **money** of every one that passeth the account, the **money** that every man is set at, and all the **money** that cometh into any man's heart to bring into the house of the LORD,"

62. 2 Kings 12:7 KJV: Then king Jehoash called for Jehoiada the priest, and the other priests, and said unto them, "Why repair ye not the breaches of the house? Now therefore receive no more **money** of your acquaintance, but deliver it for the breaches of the house."

63. 2 Kings 12:8 KJV: And the priests consented to receive no more **money** of the people, neither to repair the breaches of the house.

64. 2 Kings 12:9 KJV: But Jehoiada the priest took a chest, and bored a hole in the lid of it, and set it beside the altar, on the right side as one cometh into the house of the LORD: and the priests that kept the door put therein all the **money** that was brought into the house of the LORD.

65. 2 Kings 12:10 KJV: And it was so, when they saw that there was much money in the chest, that the king's scribe and the high priest came up, and they put up in bags, and told the **money** that was found in the house of the LORD.

66. 2 Kings 12:11 KJV: And they gave the **money**, being told, into the hands of them that did the work, that had the oversight of the house of the LORD: and they laid it out to the carpenters and builders, that wrought upon the house of the LORD

67. 2 Kings 12:13 KJV: Howbeit there were not made for the house of the LORD bowls of silver, snuffers, basins, trumpets, any vessels of gold, or vessels of silver, of the **money** that was brought into the house of the LORD:

68. 2 Kings 12:15 KJV: Moreover they reckoned not with the men, into whose hand they delivered the **money** to be bestowed on workmen: for they dealt faithfully.

69. 2 Kings 12:16 KJV: The trespass **money** and sin money was not brought into the house of the LORD: it was the priests'.

70. 2 Kings 15:20 KJV: And Menahem exacted the **money** of Israel, even of all the mighty men of wealth, of each man fifty shekels of silver, to give to the king of Assyria. So the king of Assyria turned back, and stayed not there in the land.

71. 2 Kings 22:7 KJV: Howbeit there was no reckoning made with them of the **money** that was delivered into their hand, because they dealt faithfully.

72. 2 Kings 22:9 KJV: And Shaphan the scribe came to the king, and brought the king word again, and said, "Thy servants have gathered the **money** that was found in the house, and have delivered it into the hand of them that do the work, that have the oversight of the house of the LORD."

73. 2 Kings 23:35 KJV: And Jehoiakim gave the silver and the gold to Pharaoh; but he taxed the land to give the **money** according to the commandment of Pharaoh: he exacted the silver and the

gold of the people of the land, of every one according to his taxation, to give it unto Pharaohnechoh.

74. 2 Chronicles 24:5 KJV: And he gathered together the priests and the Levites, and said to them, "Go out unto the cities of Judah, and gather of all Israel **money** to repair the house of your God from year to year, and see that ye hasten the matter." Howbeit the Levites hastened it not.

75. 2 Chronicles 24:11 KJV: Now it came to pass, that at what time the chest was brought unto the king's office by the hand of the Levites, and when they saw that there was much **money**, the king's scribe and the high priest's officer came and emptied the chest, and took it, and carried it to his place again. Thus they did day by day, and gathered money in abundance.

76. 2 Chronicles 24:14 KJV: And when they had finished it, they brought the rest of the **money** before the king and Jehoiada, whereof were made vessels for the house of the LORD, even vessels to minister, and to offer withal, and spoons, and vessels of gold and silver. And they offered burnt offerings in the house of the LORD continually all the days of Jehoiada.

77. 2 Chronicles 34:9 KJV: And when they came to Hilkiah the high priest, they delivered the **money** that was brought into the house of God, which the Levites that kept the doors had gathered of the hand of Manasseh and Ephraim, and of all the remnant of Israel, and of all Judah and Benjamin; and they returned to Jerusalem.
78. 2 Chronicles 34:14 KJV: And when they brought out the **money** that was brought into the house of the LORD, Hilkiah the priest found a book of the law of the LORD given by Moses.
79. 2 Chronicles 34:17 KJV: And they have gathered together the **money** that was found in the house of the LORD, and have delivered it into the hand of the overseers, and to the hand of the workmen.
80. Ezra 3:7 KJV: They gave **money** also unto the masons, and to the carpenters; and meat, and drink, and oil, unto them of Zidon, and to them of Tyre, to bring cedar trees from Lebanon to the sea of Joppa, according to the grant that they had of Cyrus king of Persia.
81. Ezra 7:17 KJV: That thou mayest buy speedily with this **money** bullocks, rams, lambs, with their meat offerings and their drink offerings, and offer them

upon the altar of the house of your God
which is in Jerusalem.

82. Nehemiah 5:4 KJV: There were also that
said, "We have borrowed **money** for the
king's tribute, and that upon our lands
and vineyards."

83. Nehemiah 5:10 KJV: I likewise, and my
brethren, and my servants, might exact
of them **money** and corn: I pray you, let
us leave off this usury.

84. Nehemiah 5:11 KJV: Restore, I pray
you, to them, even this day, their lands,
their vineyards, their oliveyards, and
their houses, also the hundredth part of
the **money**, and of the corn, the wine,
and the oil, that ye exact of them.

85. Esther 4:7 KJV: And Mordecai told him
of all that had happened unto him, and
of the sum of the **money** that Haman
had promised to pay to the king's
treasuries for the Jews, to destroy them.

86. Job 31:39 KJV: If I have eaten the fruits
thereof without **money**, or have caused
the owners thereof to lose their life

87. Job 42:11 KJV: Then came there unto
him all his brethren, and all his sisters,
and all they that had been of his
acquaintance before, and did eat bread
with him in his house: and they
bemoaned him, and comforted him over
all the evil that the LORD had brought

upon him: every man also gave him a piece of **money**, and every one an earring of gold.

88. Psalm 15:5 KJV: He that putteth not out his **money** to usury, nor taketh reward against the innocent. He that doeth these things shall never be moved.

89. Proverbs 7:20 KJV: He hath taken a bag of **money** with him, and will come home at the day appointed.

90. Ecclesiastes 7:12 KJV: For wisdom is a defence, and **money** is a defence: but the excellency of knowledge is, that wisdom giveth life to them that have it.

91. Ecclesiastes 10:19 KJV: A feast is made for laughter, and wine maketh merry: but **money** answereth all things.

92. Isaiah 43:24 KJV: Thou hast bought me no sweet cane with **money**, neither hast thou filled me with the fat of thy sacrifices: but thou hast made me to serve with thy sins, thou hast wearied me with thine iniquities.

93. Isaiah 52:3 KJV: For thus saith the LORD, "Ye have sold yourselves for nought; and ye shall be redeemed without money."

94. Isaiah 55:1 KJV: Ho, every one that thirsteth, come ye to the waters, and he that hath no money; come ye, buy, and eat; yea, come, buy wine and milk

without **money** and without price.

95. Isaiah 55:2 KJV: Wherefore do ye spend **money** for that which is not bread, and your labour for that which satisfieth not? Hearken diligently unto me, and eat ye that which is good, and let your soul delight itself in fatness.

96. Jeremiah 32:9 KJV: And I bought the field of Hanameel my uncle's son, that was in Anathoth, and weighed him the **money**, even seventeen shekels of silver.

97. Jeremiah 32:10 KJV: And I subscribed the evidence, and sealed it, and took witnesses, and weighed him the **money** in the balances.

98. Jeremiah 32:25 KJV: And thou hast said unto me, "O Lord GOD, Buy thee the field for **money**, and take witnesses; for the city is given into the hand of the Chaldeans."

99. Jeremiah 32:44 KJV: Men shall buy fields for **money**, and subscribe evidences, and seal them, and take witnesses in the land of Benjamin, and in the places about Jerusalem, and in the cities of Judah, and in the cities of the mountains, and in the cities of the valley, and in the cities of the south: for I will cause their captivity to return, saith the LORD.

100. Lamentations 5:4 KJV: We have

drunken our water for **money**; our wood is sold unto us.

101. Micah 3:11 KJV: The heads thereof judge for reward, and the priests thereof teach for hire, and the prophets thereof divine for **money**: yet will they lean upon the LORD, and say, Is not the LORD among us? none evil can come upon us.

102. Matthew 17:24 KJV: And when they were come to Capernaum, they that received tribute **money** came to Peter, and said, "Doth not your master pay tribute?"

103. Matthew 17:27 KJV: Notwithstanding, lest we should offend them, go thou to the sea, and cast an hook, and take up the fish that first cometh up; and when thou hast opened his mouth, thou shalt find a piece of **money**: that take, and give unto them for me and thee.

104. Matthew 22:19 KJV: Show me the tribute **money**. And they brought unto him a penny.

105. Matthew 25:18 KJV: But he that had received one went and digged in the earth, and hid his lord's **money**.

106. Matthew 25:27 KJV: Thou oughtest therefore to have put my **money** to the exchangers, and then at my coming I should have received mine own with

usury.

107. Matthew 28:12 KJV: And when they were assembled with the elders, and had taken counsel, they gave large **money** unto the soldiers

108. Matthew 28:15 KJV: So they took the **money**, and did as they were taught: and this saying is commonly reported among the Jews until this day.

109. Mark 6:8 KJV: And commanded them that they should take nothing for their journey, save a staff only; no scrip, no bread, no **money** in their purse:

110. Mark 12:41 KJV: And Jesus sat over against the treasury, and beheld how the people cast **money** into the treasury: and many that were rich cast in much.

111. Mark 14:11 KJV: And when they heard it, they were glad, and promised to give him **money**. And he sought how he might conveniently betray him.

112. Luke 9:3 KJV: And he said unto them, "Take nothing for your journey, neither staves, nor scrip, neither bread, neither **money**; neither have two coats apiece."

113. Luke 19:15 KJV: And it came to pass, that when he was returned, having received the kingdom, then he commanded these servants to be called unto him, to whom he had given the **money**, that he might know how much

every man had gained by trading.

114. Luke 19:23 KJV: Wherefore then gavest not thou my **money** into the bank, that at my coming I might have required mine own with usury?

115. Luke 22:5 KJV: And they were glad, and covenanted to give him **money**.

116. John 2:14 KJV: And found in the temple those that sold oxen and sheep and doves, and the changers of **money** sitting.

117. John 2:15 KJV: And when he had made a scourge of small cords, he drove them all out of the temple, and the sheep, and the oxen; and poured out the changers' **money**, and overthrew the tables.

118. Acts 4:37 KJV: Having land, sold it, and brought the **money**, and laid it at the apostles' feet.

119. Acts 7:16 KJV: And were carried over into Sychem, and laid in the sepulchre that Abraham bought for a sum of **money** of the sons of Emmor the father of Sychem.

120. Acts 8:18 KJV: And when Simon saw that through laying on of the apostles' hands the Holy Ghost was given, he offered them **money**,

121. Acts 8:20 KJV: But Peter said unto

him, "Thy money perish with thee, because thou hast thought that the gift of God may be purchased with **money**."

122. Acts 24:26 KJV: He hoped also that **money** should have been given him of Paul, that he might loose him: wherefore he sent for him the oftener, and communed with him.

123. 1 Timothy 6:10 KJV: For the love of **money** is the root of all evil: which while some coveted after, they have erred from the faith, and pierced themselves through with many sorrows.

Index

LaVergne, TN USA
08 December 2010
207926LV00002B/11/A